Cool, Confident and Strong

52 Power Moves for Girls

2nd Printing

By: Cassandra Mack

I0616427

Authors Choice Press
New York Lincoln Shanghai

Cool, Confident and Strong
52 Power Moves for Girls

Copyright © 2005, 2007 by Cassandra Mack

Authors Choice Press
an imprint of iUniverse, Inc.

iUniverse books may be ordered through booksellers or by contacting:

iUniverse
2021 Pine Lake Road, Suite 100
Lincoln, NE 68512
www.iuniverse.com
1-800-Authors (1-800-288-4677)

Originally published by Strategies for Empowered Living Inc.

Because of the dynamic nature of the Internet, any Web addresses or links contained in this book may have changed since publication and may no longer be valid.

The views expressed in this work are solely those of the author and do not necessarily reflect the views of the publisher, and the publisher hereby disclaims any responsibility for them.

ISBN: 978-0-595-47560-5

Printed in the United States of America

Contents

A Message To The Mothers of Adolescent Girls, 5

A Message To Adolescent Girls, 7

Power Move #1. Love Yourself Just the Way You Are, 8

Power Move #2. Cherish Your Girlfriends, 10

Power Move #3. Dare To Be You, 11

Power Move #4. Discover What Brings You Joy, 12

Power Move #5. Unlock The Key To High Self-esteem, 14

Power Move #6. Follow Your Own Lead, 17

Power Move #7. Look Hot Without Taking Off Your Clothes, 18

Power Move #8. Be Diligent About Your Grooming and Hygiene, 21

Power Move #9. Be A Clear Communicator, 24

Power Move #10. Practice Reflective Listening, 26

Power Move #11. Don't Obsess Over What Other People Think, 28

Power Move #12. Get Physical, 29

Power Move #13. Don't Keep Painful Feelings Inside, 30

Power Move #14. Put An End to Petty Jealousy, 31

Power Move #15. Cut Your Mom Some Slack, 32

Power Move #16. Dads Are Important Too, 33

Power Move #17. Choose Your Friends Wisely, 34

Power Move #18. Don't Let Peer Pressure Get The Best of You, 35

Power Move #19. Make Education A Top Priority, 38

Power Move #20. Don't Get Suckered Into Sex, 39

Power Move #21. It's OK Not to Have A Boyfriend, 41

Power Move #22. Be Smart About Dating, 42

Power Move #23. Don't Hide Him From Your Parents, 44

Power Move #24. Heed the Warning Signs of An Abusive Relationship, 46

Power Move #25. Watch Out for Older Guys, 49

Power Move #26. Don't Ditch Your Girlfriends for A Guy, 51

Power Move #27. Don't Get Involved With Guys Headed for Trouble, 52

Power Move #28. Leave Her Boyfriend Alone, 53

Power Move #29. Trust You'll Bounce Back From A Break-up, 54

Power Move # 30. Try Not to Get Stressed Out By Cliques, 56

Power Move #31. Don't Use Friendship As A Weapon, 57

Power Move #32. Be Careful Not to Let Your Friends Do Your Thinking for You, 58

Power Move #33. Know That Rainy Days Won't Last Forever, 59

Power Move #34. Learn to Say No, 60

Power Move #35. Don't Take Everything So Personally, 61

Power Move #36. Look Inside Yourself for Happiness, 62

Power Move #37. Express Yourself, 63

Power Move #38. Trust Your Intuition, 64

Power Move #39. When You Don't Know What Else to Do Pray, 65

Power Move #40. Keep A Journal, 66

Power Move #41. Make The World A Better Place To Live, 67

Power Move #42. If A Friend's In Serious Trouble Get Help, 68

Power Move #43. Cultivate Your Interests, 69

Power Move #44. Don't Place Limitations On Yourself, 71

Power Move #45. Earn Your Own Money, 73

Power Move #46. Be A Penny Pincher, 74

Power Move #47. Let Go Of the Need To Be Perfect, 75

Power Move #48. Make Room for New Friends, 77

Power Move #49. Try Something New, 78

Power Move #50. Follow Your Dreams, 79

Power Move #51. Learn From Your Sheroes, 81

Power Move #52. Remember That Life Is A Journey, 83

Discussion Guide, 85

Tips for Starting Your Own Mother and Daughter Reading Group, 92

Suggested Reading and Websites for Teenage Girls, 95

About the Author, 96

Other Books By Cassandra Mack, 97

A Message To The Mothers
of Adolescent Girls

As a woman, a mother, an older sister and a former adolescent girl, I believe that it is our task as adult women to give every teenage girl the space she needs to realize that her struggles and challenges are not unique, that she is not alone in her experiences and that moments of doubt and insecurity are a normal part of adolescent development. We have all been there.

It is important for young women to have as many avenues as possible to receive positive messages about themselves and discover their inner power. This is how girls learn to develop a healthy sense of self as well as make decisions that respect their values and boundaries.

Girls need to learn how to feel capable, valuable and confident, and they need our help. Girls need to learn how to stop basing their social identities on media images or what other people think, and they need our help. Girls must be encouraged to embrace their strengths and stand up for themselves, and they need our help. This means providing girls not only with nurturing, support and love but also accurate information around the challenges they face and a skill set to maneuver through this tumultuous time.

Cool, Confident and Strong candidly explores many of the issues that confront girls as they struggle toward womanhood. From body image to boys, peer pressure to parents, dealing with painful secrets to surviving cliques, throughout these pages you will find that there is a place where girls can go to get reaffirmation and sound advice.

I strongly encourage you to read *Cool, Confident and Strong* then go through the discussion guide on pages 85 through 91 with your daughter. The *Cool,*

Confident and Strong discussion guide was developed to begin the process of breaking down walls between mothers and daughters, bridge generational gaps and initiate open and honest dialogue about the many issues that impact today's adolescent girls.

I believe that you will find the book and the discussion guide quite helpful. After reading the book and going through the discussion guide with your daughter or mother/daughter group, please e-mail me at: **teenpowermove@aol.com** to let me know how things went. Please make sure to write, *"Cool, Confident and Strong Discussion Guide"* in the subject section of your e-mail. I look forward to hearing from you.

A Message To Adolescent Girls

Growing up, I often wished I had an older sister. Someone who would encourage me to go for my dreams, let me know that it's ok to just be myself, understand me when I felt misunderstood and give me advice on guys, school, dealing with friends, getting along with my mother and coping with tough times. She would share her experiences with me and offer words of wisdom so that I could get through my teen years a little easier.

In my workshops for teenage girls I meet so many young women who feel the same way – who wish they had a supportive, older, sister to help them navigate this tumultuous time in their lives. *Cool, Confident and Strong* can be like your big sister providing you with encouragement and guidance so that you can arm yourself with practical information about topics that matter to you.

Cool, Confident and Strong offers fifty-two power moves on things like: boys, friendship, parents, school, cool ways to earn extra money, surviving cliques, communication, self-image and so much more. The book is set up so that you can go directly to the topic that you want to focus on. If you don't know what to do about a particular situation, go to the power move that deals with that issue and apply the advice to your situation.

The possibilities for you are endless, but in order to grow into your full potential, you need more than a "girl power" slogan. You need to know how to find your own voice and make wise choices. *Cool, Confident and Strong* will provide you with the tools you need to celebrate yourself, reflect on your life and take action so that you can become the amazing young woman you are meant to be.

Power Move #1

Love Yourself Just the Way You Are

One of my favorite songs is a song by India Arie entitled, "Video." In this song she sings about how she doesn't look like the idealized girls in popular music videos, but that she's beautiful none-the-less. Contrary to the images of beauty that are often portrayed on television and in magazines, there is no such thing as the perfect kind of beauty because we are all beautiful in our own unique way. The key to being your most beautiful self is learning how to accentuate your natural attributes so that the real you can shine through.

The most disturbing thing that a girl can do to herself is to pick herself apart because she doesn't fit the media's cookie-cutter image of beauty. The simple fact is the more you celebrate and accept the way you look, the more beautiful you become. This really is true. Haven't you met people who didn't fit the conventional definition of beauty but something about them made them irresistibly attractive? So you see, it's not about fitting an ideal; it's about celebrating your uniqueness and playing up your best features. When you carry yourself like the amazing girl that you are, you will radiate the kind of beauty that will make people stop and take notice of you.

It took me a long time to grasp this concept, because we live in a culture that idolizes the ultra thin. And for most of my teenage and young adult years, I've struggled with my weight. I always thought that since I was full-figured I couldn't wear what everyone else was wearing. But as soon as I learned to embrace my full-figure and work with the package that God gave me, I discovered my own unique style and people took notice. As I felt more attractive, I became more attractive – and the same thing goes for you.

Instead of trying to measure up to an unrealistic image or obsessing over what you believe to be your flaws, start embracing the things that are unique about you and know that you were perfectly designed by God.

Power Move #2

Cherish Your Girlfriends

There is nothing like having close girlfriends who you can talk to, hang out with and lean on when you're feeling down. Your girlfriends can make the good times better and the bad times easier to bear. It is important that you cherish your female friends, because far too often girls viciously compete with one another even if they are friends. Girls compete for attention from guys, popularity and acceptance from peers. Sometimes they even gossip about each other, backstab one another and change alliances at the drop of a hat.

Petty rivalry among friends defeats the purpose of friendship. True friends support each other and are happy when the other succeeds at something. They show each other that they care by: being kind, trustworthy, encouraging and supportive. True friends do not gossip about one another or take each other for granted.

Your girlfriends can enrich your life in many ways. If you are fortunate enough to have true friends, don't take these friendships lightly. Let your girlfriends know that you appreciate them. Give your best friend a call, send her an e-mail or drop her a note that says, "I value your friendship." When you cherish your girlfriends, you'll develop unbreakable sister-bonds.

Today, think about all the ways that you can show your girlfriends that you cherish them.

Power Move #3

Dare to Be You

There is a simple secret to having a healthy sense of self–esteem ... dare to be you. Just being yourself will make your life more happy, healthy and whole. During adolescence, you are at a stage of life where you are pulling way from your parents, trying out new things, opening your mind to new ideas and asking yourself lots of deep, reflective questions in order to figure out who you are. This helps you to develop a positive identity. Part of finding out who you are means: figuring out your likes and dislikes, building friendships with different kinds of people and getting clear about what you want out of life. The more comfortable you are with yourself, the more you'll be able to develop a positive identity.

Sometimes you may find yourself changing your personality in order to get people to like you. But this is never a good idea because you can't put up a front forever and it takes too much work to be fake. Some people believe that if they change who they are, then their friends will accept them. But this is simply not true because there are some people who will not like you no matter what you do. And you don't need friends like that anyway.

The wonderful thing about being yourself is, no one can do it better than you. Be bold. Be courageous. And most of all; be you.

Today, create a list of things that you can do to let the real you shine through.

Power Move #4

Discover What Brings You Joy

What are some of your favorite things to do? Discovering what brings you joy is one of the keys to having a happy life. Our society often equates happiness with money, popularity and other external things. But these things cannot bring you true happiness. If you know what brings you joy and you do the things that lift your spirits then you will live a happy life.

Here are some of the things that bring me joy:

- Reading a good book.

- Dancing to a great song.

- Singing and making up songs.

- Watching a funny movie.

- Writing poetry.

- Getting together with friends and family.

- Praying and listening to gospel music.

Go to a quiet place and write down some of the things that bring you joy.

_____

_____

_____

_____

_____

What did you discover about yourself as a result of writing down the things that bring you joy? My guess is, you found out that it's not the external things that make you happy like: having lots of clothes, being popular or having lots of money. I'll bet it was the little things like: watching a beautiful sunrise, traveling to a far away place, hanging out with friends or spending time with family.

Over the next few days pay attention to the people around you who are truly happy. It's probably not their money, status or material possessions that bring them happiness, it's the contentment that they feel on the inside and the love they receive from friends and family. When you follow your heart and do what brings you joy, you'll discover the secret to happiness.

Power Move #5

Unlock the Key to High Self-esteem

Self-esteem refers to how you think and feel about yourself. It is your belief about how valuable and worthy you are as a person. When you have high self-esteem, you feel good about yourself and have a healthy appreciation for your best qualities. When you have low self-esteem, you feel badly about yourself and you are unable to see your positive qualities.

A big part of your self-esteem comes from the messages that you receive about yourself over time. These messages can come from your family, friends, teachers or the media. They can even come from you – your thoughts and the things that you say to yourself when no one else is around.

It's important to keep in mind that self-esteem is something that we have to work on continually because girls and women are constantly bombarded with messages that can make us doubt ourselves.

So how do you unlock the key to high self-esteem? You unlock the key to high self-esteem in five ways: you choose to think positively, you surround yourself with positive people, you remind yourself that you have what it takes to go far in life, you participate in activities that you enjoy and you put your best foot forward in all that you do.

In my book, *Young, Gifted and Doing It: 52 Power Moves for Teens,* I guide readers through an exercise where I ask them to replace negative self-talk with more positive messages. I think you'll benefit from this same exercise. For every negative thought that you have, I'd like you to replace it with a more positive realistic message. Below are some examples of

14

how you can replace a negative message with a positive realistic one.

Negative Message
I'm so stupid. I'll never pass this test.
Positive, Realistic Message
I am bright. If I study hard and apply myself I can pass this test.
Negative Message
I'm not as pretty as the other girls.
Positive, Realistic Message
I am a good person I am beautiful inside and out.

Negative Message

_____
_____
_____

Positive, Realistic Message

_____
_____
_____

Negative Message

_____
_____
_____

Positive, Realistic Message

_____
_____
_____

Repeat the positive messages regularly so that you can get in the habit of speaking positively about yourself.

My Plan for Boosting My Self-esteem

1. Positive Self-talk
I will try not to put myself down. Instead I will build myself up by acknowledging what's good about me and what's good about my life. These are some of the positive things that I can say to myself when I feel tempted to put myself down.

_____

_____

2. Surrounding Myself With Positive People
I can surround myself with positive people who support me and bring out the best in me. Here are the names of at least two people who I can call on when I need support and encouragement.

_____

_____

3. Things That Remind Me That I Have What It Takes To Make It
These are the things that I can do to remind myself that I have what it takes to make it.

_____

_____

4. Activities That I Enjoy
These are the activities that I enjoy.

_____

_____

5. Putting My Best Foot Forward
This is what I will do to show that I am committed to putting my best foot forward.

_____

_____

Power Move #6

Follow Your Own Lead

Have you ever found yourself doing something that you really didn't want to do, just because all of your friends were doing it? How did you feel afterward? I'll bet that you felt pretty bad. Maybe you let a secret slip, made fun of a less popular girl, took a sip of beer or smoked marijuana; even though you always thought that you were the type of person who would never do anything that went against your values.

Nobody's perfect. But it is important that you pay attention to the thoughts that run through your head whenever you are tempted to stray from your values. Even if you strongly believe in your values, you may still stray from them if you are pressured hard enough. Since you're still learning and growing it's hard to say that you'll never do anything that goes against your beliefs if the pressure is really on. Because during the teen years peer pressure is at an all time high. This is why it is so important that you figure out what your values are and that you try to stand by them no matter how much pressure you are under.

Sometimes we get so caught up in wanting to be accepted that we do things that go against what we know to be right. And usually when it's all said and done we feel badly. The best way to avoid feeling badly after you have made a decision is to make decisions that are consistent with the positive values that were instilled in you growing up. And know for yourself that no matter how far you go, if the situation doesn't feel right, you have the right to change your mind. Follow your own lead and you will never go wrong.

Power Move #7

Look Hot Without Taking Off Your Clothes

We live in a culture where dressing scantily and provocatively seems to be the new norm. Television commercials are filled with young women wearing next to nothing selling everything from cars and bikes to pretzels and chips. Music videos feature girls in string bikinis and thongs being reduced to mere sex objects. And entertainers like Britney Spears and Lil Kim seem to be competing for the skimpiest outfit of the year award. It's enough to make a girl feel like she doesn't measure up unless she's wearing the shortest, tightest and hoochiest outfit that she can find.

There is nothing wrong with looking cute and sassy. But you can look cute and sassy without taking off all your clothes. Why not follow some of the fashion trends while hooking it up with your own unique style. Your clothing speaks to others long before they have an opportunity to get to know you. And although you may not want to give off a message that says, "I'm easy." Like it or not, people may form this kind of opinion of you if you dress too provocatively. And while you should not obsess over what other people think about you, there are some instances where it does matter like: a job interview, a college interview or meeting someone else's parents.

Dress for the occasion. Wear clothes that make you feel confident and comfortable. There are lots of great clothes that are stylish, affordable and appropriate for your age. The media tries to encourage girls to look and act older than they are. But you're too smart to let the media do your thinking for you. Make your fashion choices based on your own unique

18

style. Here are some helpful tips for dressing in style on a budget.

- ***Volunteer to Model for A Department Store or Community Fashion Show***

Some department stores use real people models to showcase their new fashions. Sometimes the models even get to keep an outfit or purchase it at a discounted price. Also modeling for a church or community sponsored fashion show can be another great way to earn cool stuff. Ask around and see, you never know.

- ***Shop In Your Girlfriend's Closet***

If you are like most young women, I'll bet that your closet is full of clothes that you've never worn or haven't worn in ages; outfits that you hang on to telling yourself that someday you'll wear them. Why not get together with a group of friends and have a clothing swap. Tell all your girls to go through their closets, dresser drawers and shoe boxes and bring in stuff that they haven't worn in a long time or don't plan on wearing any more. Maybe one of your friends has a skirt that goes perfectly with that funky blouse you got for your birthday. Perhaps that jacket your mother bought you that you absolutely hate will go perfectly with your best friend's suede boots. And whatever items are left over can be donated to a shelter. Shopping in your girlfriend's closet is the perfect way to get new clothes without spending a dime.

- ***Learn How to Sew***

Learning how to sew is a great way to dress fashionably without spending a lot of money. Get your grandma's old sewing machine out and ask her to show you some basic stitches. Find out if there is a sewing class in your neighborhood and sign up for it. Once you get really good at it, you may want to think about starting a part time business making outfits for your friends.

* **_Go to Thrift and Consignment Shops_**
Believe it or not, you can find some great items at thrift and consignment shops if you look with a discerning eye. Create your own look by trying on different items then buy what looks good on you.

* **_Go to Outlets_**
The wonderful thing about outlets is they offer your favorite brands at discounted prices. Visit the outlet stores in your town and scope the clearance racks for additional bargains.

Power Move #8

Be Diligent About Your Grooming and Hygiene

In the previous power move we talked about how to look hot without taking off your clothes. However, looking good begins with proper grooming and hygiene habits. Loving and caring for your teeth, body and skin, says that you care enough about yourself to take pride in your appearance. Below are some basic hygiene and grooming tips.

1. Caring for Your Face
When caring for your face, it is important to wash your face when you get up in the morning and before you go to bed. Use moisturizer after washing your face and if you wear make-up remember to wash it off.

2. Caring for Your Ears
Be careful not to let ear wax build up. Get a clean damp cloth and wash in and around your ears. Do not use a q-tip; you can rupture your eardrum.

3. Caring for Your Teeth and Mouth
Dentists' say that you should brush and floss after every meal. Oftentimes you won't be able to brush after every meal but it's important that you remember to brush your teeth when you wake up and before you go to bed.

4. Caring for Your Nose

You should clean and check your nose everyday. After all you wouldn't want someone else to point out that you've got a big boogie hanging from your nose.

5. Caring for Your Body

You need to take a bath or shower everyday, preferably in the morning. And don't forget to moisturize. Some girls bathe at night and do a quick wash-up in the morning. But because the female body is capable of producing a strong and sometimes not so pleasant odor, it's a good idea to start the day off fresh.

6. Caring for Your Hands and Feet

Be sure to clean underneath your fingernails and clip those toenails. Wash your hands and feet thoroughly. Learn how to do your own manicures and pedicures. It will save you a fortune.

7. Caring for Your Vaginal Area

It's important to properly care for your vaginal area. Wash yourself thoroughly. During your menstrual cycle, shower regularly and change your sanitary napkins every two to three hours or more if you bleed very heavily. Pay attention to any strong odors or discolorations. And see a gynecologist regularly. If you're not seeing one now, talk to your mom or one of your aunts and have them take you.

8. Caring for Your Hair

Wash and condition your hair once a week. Trim your ends every eight to ten weeks. If you have a dry scalp, give yourself periodic hot oil treatments. Find hairstyles that flatter your face. And remember there's no such thing as good hair. If it's on your head, then it is good.

9. Caring for Your Clothes
Always make sure that your clothes are neat and clean. Iron your clothing. Check your clothing for stains and odors.

10.   Smelling Sweet
Don't forget to use underarm deodorant. Don't over do it with the perfume. Never spray perfume in your vaginal area it can cause irritation or an infection.

Power Move #9

Be A Clear Communicator

Good communication skills can make a big difference when it comes to getting along with others. A good way to become a clear communicator is to express your feelings using "I" language. Most people use "You" language then wonder why the other person can't see their point of view. "You" language sounds something like this: *You make me so upset. You are such a backstabber. I can't stand it when you get around Felicia. You act like I don't exist.*

The problem with "You" language is it puts the other person on the defensive. And when you put people on the defensive they will attack back or completely tune you out. A more effective way to express your feelings is to use "I" language. An "I" statement sounds something like this: *I feel hurt and left out whenever Felicia comes around. I notice that the two of you go off into your own conversation and leave me out. It makes me wonder if we are still best friends. I need to know that I won't feel like an outsider when Felicia hangs out with us.*

It is important for you to know that using "I" language won't guarantee that the other person will agree with your point of view or that the situation will turn out the way you want it to. But it will enable you to express yourself clearly and completely without making the other person feel like you are attacking them.

Take a few moments to turn these "You" statements into "I" statements.

1. You Statement
You are such a flirt. Whenever a guy comes around, you start acting all loose and conceited.

I Statement:

_____

_____

_____

2. You Statement
You have such a big mouth. You are clueless when it comes to keeping a secret. You really need to stop talking so much.

I Statement:

_____

_____

_____

3. You Statement
Mom, you never let me do anything. You're so controlling. You never let me hang out with my friends. I might as well be in prison.

I Statement:

_____

_____

_____

Power Move #10

Practice Reflective Listening

If there is someone in your life who you constantly argue with or get into power struggles with, it might be well worth the effort to try a little reflective listening. With reflective listening you really try to take in what the other person is saying, then repeat what you think they said in order to ensure that you understood them. This technique makes communication flow more smoothly. If you want to become a reflective listener, try these five simple steps.

1. Listen closely to what the other person is trying to say and don't interrupt them or drift off to think about what you are going to say next.

2. Don't just listen to the words that the person uses, pay attention to his or her tone of voice, facial expressions and body language. This will help you to really get in tune with what the other person is saying to you.

3. Take a few minutes to collect your thoughts and take in everything you felt and everything the other person said.

4. Paraphrase what the other person said by repeating it back to them as best as you can.

5. Be calm and state what's on your mind. Don't give off a negative attitude.

By practicing reflective listening not only do you become a better listener, you become a better communicator as well.

Power Move #11

Don't Obsess Over What Other People Think

As an adolescent girl you are often told not to worry about what other people think and that if you have positive self-esteem and your own set of values, then what other people think shouldn't matter to you. This is good advice, but it's not as easy as it sounds. Even if you are confident with high self-esteem occasionally you can still get caught up in worrying about what your peers thinks, because you are at a stage in your life where fitting in with your friends and classmates is important to you.

Although you may find yourself wondering about what other people think, try not to obsess over it. Opinions are like noses, everybody has one. And when you put too much emphasis on what people think, you will live your life trying to keep up with the Jones's or you'll find yourself saying and doing things that completely go against your beliefs.

It's been said that small minds talk about people, while great minds talk about ideas. So whenever you base a decision on what someone else thinks, you are letting small-minded people get the best of you.

Try to stop obsessing over what other people think. In the end people who matter, won't criticize and people who criticize don't matter.

Power Move # 12

Get Physical

Did you know that there is a direct correlation between physical activity and your general health and well-being? Girls who participate in sports or some form of regular physical activity tend to be more confident, assertive and less stressed than those who do not. Incorporating physical fitness activities into your weekly schedule is a great way to become more fit and feel good about yourself. Whether you play volleyball, dance, jump rope or take an exercise class, regular physical activity leads to an enhanced quality of life.

When I was in high school, I hated gym. I was what you would call a couch potato. But the older I got, the more I realized the importance of incorporating some form of physical activity into my schedule. The best time to start taking care of your body is now while you are young and healthy. Below is a list of physical fitness activities. Circle the one or ones that you participate in or would like to participate in.

> ➤ Jump Rope
> ➤ Golf
> ➤ Volley Ball
> ➤ Basket Ball
> ➤ Bike Riding
> ➤ Tennis
> ➤ Dance
> ➤ Swimming
> ➤ Fencing
> ➤ Gymnastics
> ➤ Aerobics
> ➤ Walking/Jogging/Running

Power Move # 13

Don't Keep Painful Feelings Inside

Sometimes keeping painful feelings to yourself can make your problem seem bigger than it is. Or, it can make you feel like you are the only one who is going through your situation. When you keep painful feelings bottled up inside for a long time, you begin to believe that you are all alone and that no one else can ever understand what you are going through.

Don't let yourself feel this way. There are people all around you who care about you and who want to help. But if they don't know what you are going through, then they cannot help you. It's not always easy to talk about your problems or let someone in on a painful secret, but it is important that you reach out for support. Sometimes it's a good idea to start by writing your feelings down in a journal. This way, you don't have to worry about finding the right words to say. After you write your feelings down the next step is to talk to someone about your situation. Talk to someone you trust and if you don't get the help you need, talk to someone else. Just keep talking.

It is difficult enough to be in emotional pain so it's important that you do not let your feelings overwhelm you. Reaching out to others is a cool move. Not only will it help you to feel better, you will feel more empowered and in control of your life.

There is something very healing about getting painful feelings off your chest, especially if the person who is listening to you can give you some sound advice. Your school may have a counselor who you can talk to. Or maybe you can talk to one of your teachers. If you are in any kind of emotional pain, take a deep breath and tell someone about it.

Power Move #14

Put An End To Petty Jealousy

Back when I was in the eighth grade I used to be jealous of one of my classmates. I thought she was prettier than I was, had nicer clothes and was more popular. And whenever I measured myself against her I felt like I always came up short. And the truth is I did fall short, because I was so busy worrying about what she had and how many more people liked her, that I neglected to focus on my own strengths and talents and appreciate my own beauty and circle of friends. Instead of doing my own thing and focusing on developing myself I was caught up in her world trying to be like her or out do her.

When I finally started to focus my attention on me and appreciate what I had to offer I lived a happier life. I joined the drama club. I made up songs with my friends. To tell you the truth, I just enjoyed being me. When I made the decision to stop secretly competing with my classmate and focus on me I was able to put an end to petty jealousy.

Instead of competing with your friends, discover what your special gifts are and nurture them. Appreciate what you have to offer. The more you appreciate and accept yourself, the more you will realize that there is no need to be jealous of anyone else. Why? Because you will start to see how special and gifted you are in your own right. Today, appreciate yourself and make the decision to put an end to petty jealousy.

Power Move # 15

Cut Your Mom Some Slack

You may have noticed that since you became a teenager, you are having a tougher time getting along with your mom. You probably don't even know why the two of you argue so much. But one thing is certain: you fight much more than you ever did before.

Something happens between a mother and her daughter, when the daughter reaches adolescence. A power struggle often occurs with you pulling away from your mother in order to find your own way and gain greater independence while your mother holds on tighter because she feels like she is losing her little girl. This power struggle is completely normal and happens to just about every mother and daughter. But try to remember that things are just as hard for your mom as they are for you. In her eyes you are growing and changing so quickly that she doesn't know what to do. In your eyes you just want her to leave you alone so that you can do your own thing.

Even though you are starting to find your own way, don't shut your mom out because you still need her. Maybe not so much to protect you, but to guide you and show you what it takes to become a responsible and well-adjusted young woman. So show your mom some love by cutting her a little slack.

The constant fighting won't last forever. Believe it or not, there will probably come a time when you and your mom will be closer than ever before. Although your mom may seem a bit overbearing (ok maybe a lot) keep in mind that your mom is doing the best that she can and she really does want what's best for you.

Power Move #16

Dads Are Important Too

When I was writing this power move, I talked to lots of different girls to find out what kind of relationships they had with their fathers. Their responses were so varied. Some had close relationships with their fathers. Others had strained relationships. Still others had no contact with their fathers at all. But the one thing they all had in common was, no matter what kind of relationship they had with their fathers – emotionally available or totally absent from their lives – they were all impacted by their fathers. This is why I say that dads are important too.

Whether you realize it or not, fathers are an important part of a girl's development. Your father is your first image of manhood. He models for you what it means to be a man. He teaches you how a woman should be treated. If you have a close relationship with your father then you have a positive image of manhood. If you do not have a relationship with your father, then that image is often shattered.

If you live with your father or have some sort of contact with him, try to make him an intricate part of your life. He can give you advice from a male's point of view, help you to better understand how to deal with males and he can help you to better understand your mother since he knew her before you did.

Power Move #17

Choose Your Friends Wisely

So many things go into building a friendship. Usually friendships start out because you and the other person have fun together, participate in similar activities or like the same things. I've been thinking about this a lot lately because so many teens write to me about different situations involving their friends. And what I have come to know is that sometimes the people who are cool to hang out with don't always make the best friends. What is most important in building a friendship is that your friends accept you for you and that they positively contribute to your life.

Choose friends not only on the basis of whether or not they are ok to hang out with; make sure that they accept you for you, genuinely care abut you and are supportive of you. Put some distance between yourself and friends who are headed down the wrong path.

Sometimes you may find yourself in a situation where someone who you consider to be a friend puts you down, behaves in ways that make you feel uncomfortable or acts distant toward you. When this happens sometimes the best thing that you can do for yourself as well as your friend is to pull away.

Sometimes friends just grow apart and there are no words to explain why the two of you are headed in different directions. Pulling away from a friend is never easy, but it can give you the time and space to think through your situation and see if it's worth the effort to try to rebuild the friendship. And if things do not work out, it gives you the space to make new friends who you will have more in common with.

Power Move # 18

Don't Let Peer Pressure Get The Best of You

Sometimes just to be popular and fit in with the crowd, you may find yourself doing things that you really don't want to do. Many people will tell you that if you are clear about your values then you won't give into negative peer pressure. But this is not always true. You can have your own set of values and still make a bad decision because you're only human and during the teen years peer pressure is at an all time high.

This is why you've got to not only have a clear set of values, you also have to know how to assess potentially harmful situations and come up with a plan for keeping yourself out of trouble when the pressure's on. One of the best ways to develop the skills to resist negative peer pressure is to practice hypothetical pressure situations with your parents or another mature adult. For example, think about your friends at school and in your social circle and recall different situations that they have been in. Go over some of these scenarios with an adult and practice different ways that you might handle these situations if they happen to you. Rehearse what you might say and do if you were being pressured to do something that could result in a negative consequence. Ask your parents to give you more ways that you can handle yourself when faced with tense situations and practice until your responses come naturally.

Here is a four-step refusal strategy that you can use when you are faced with negative peer pressure.

Step 1. Find Out What's About to Go Down

Whenever you are being pressured to do something that could place you or someone else in harm's way, the first thing you need to do is find out exactly what it is that the person or people want you to do. Be as specific as possible. You need to ask questions like: *What exactly are you going to do? What specifically are you asking me to do? Who else is going to be there? What will the other people be doing? How do you know for sure that we won't get in trouble or that none of us will have any regrets?*

You can re-word these questions so they reflect the way you and your peers normally speak to each other. What's most important is that you ask the kinds of questions that will enable you to gather enough information to make a smart decision.

Step 2. Find Out Who's Going to Be Involved

Finding out who will be involved allows you to not only assess the situation more carefully, it also will give you a clear picture of the character and values of the other kids. Further, you can pretty much predict whether or not these are the kind of people who are on the wrong path. Some of the questions you may want to ask yourself are: *What do I really know about these people? Do these kids usually get into trouble at home or school? Do these kids smoke, drink, do drugs, start fights, cut class or do anything else that signals that they are headed for trouble? Are these the kind of friends that my parents or other people who care about me would approve of?*

Step 3. Weigh the Pros and Cons

If you're still undecided about what to do, weigh the pros and cons of participating in the activity. This is a very important step, because you'll have to dig deep inside yourself and think about everything that could possibly happen if you give into the pressure.

36

You need to ask yourself: *What's the worst that could happen? Will the people who care about me be disappointed in me? Will I be disappointed in myself? Could someone else get hurt? Can I live with the consequences?*

Asking yourself these kinds of questions will allow you to carefully think through all of the worst case scenarios as well as reflect on your values so that you won't make a decision that you might later regret.

Step 4. Do the Right Thing and Stand Firm In Your Decision

Deep inside you know what's right, so do the right thing. Some kids use their age as an excuse to go along with the crowd and participate in negativity. But by now you know the difference between what's right and what's wrong. Besides you are too smart to make excuses. It may not be easy, but you can do the right thing and stand firm in your decision. And no matter how far you go you always have the right to back out and change your mind. Remember, you are too smart to let others negatively influence you.

Power Move #19

Make Education A Top Priority

Here's some simple advice that will do you a world of good: Make education your #1 priority. You don't have to be a nerd or a bookworm to follow this advice, you simply have to make up your mind to be disciplined and focused. Get a journal and write down at least three things that you will do differently starting tomorrow to focus more on your education. Make a vow to study more, participate more in class and bring your grades up.

Think about ways that you can grow more and turn yourself into a powerhouse of knowledge. Find out what your teachers want and expect from you and take the initiative to give it to them.

Excelling in school takes work. Some people retain information easier than others. And a few people can maintain high grades without a lot of study. But most of us have to apply ourselves in order to excel. If you want to succeed in life, start by succeeding in school. Today, spend one additional hour studying or reading. And think about what else you can do to make sure that your education remains a top priority.

Power Move #20

Don't Get Suckered Into Sex

Sex is everywhere. It's on television and in the movies. You hear about it on the radio and read about it in newspapers and magazines. You've probably even had conversations with your girlfriends about who is doing it and who is not, who kissed a guy and who went as far as having a guy touch her breasts. These kinds of conversations are not uncommon among girls your age. I had them when I was your age and so did your mom whether she chooses to admit it to you or not.

Now is the time to start thinking about how you are going to handle yourself when you start dating. It's important that you set standards for yourself, respect your body and make guys respect it by not allowing them to touch you in ways that push you too far or demean you.

Many adults are not comfortable talking with teenagers about sex, especially girls. But it is a subject that must be discussed so that you can stand strong when you are faced with the pressure to engage in sexual activities. Often adults will tell you: "Just Don't Do It." And while this is good advice, you need more than a slogan to learn how to respect your body and make others respect it. You need to know how to set clear boundaries and keep yourself out of situations that might tempt you to go too far.

You don't have to feel bad about your curiosity. Being curious is natural. What's important for you to understand is that you do not have to act on your curiosity or your desires. The longer you hold off on sex the better. The longer you wait, the more time you have to develop your values and enjoy the benefits of being a virgin like: a high reputation, respect from others, not being at risk for sexually transmitted diseases, not getting pregnant and the high self-esteem that comes with treating yourself like a young queen. And even if guys never say or show it, they will respect you more in the long run because they'll know how highly you think of yourself. And this makes you more desirable.

As a teenage girl, it is important for you to know that most teenage boys will say and do just about anything to get girls to make out with them, let them feel you up and have sex with them. But you are too smart to sell yourself short. Sometimes guys will tell you that they love you when they do not or they'll tell you that everyone else is doing it. And you know that's not true. Make guys respect you by respecting yourself. And if you decide to go out with a guy, make sure he's willing to wait.

Throughout your life, you will be faced with many decisions concerning sex. You'll be placed in situations where you will have to decide how far to go and how far not to go. The best way to ensure that you don't go too far is to make a special vow to yourself to wait. By making a vow (a sacred promise to yourself) you will be more in control of your life and you'll be better able to stand up for your values. Today, make the choice to hold off on sex. After all: aren't you worth the wait?

Power Move #21

It's OK Not to Have A Boyfriend

Girls are constantly given the message that they are not complete unless they have a boyfriend. Whenever you turn on the TV you see commercials or shows with couples walking hand in hand looking so much in love. And if you pick up a copy of YM or Cosmo Girl magazine you'll read headlines that say things like: *"How to get him to notice you."* Or, *"How to get the guy of your dreams to ask you out in six easy steps."* It's enough to make a girl feel like there's something wrong with her if she doesn't have a boyfriend or at least a guy that she's interested in.

Believe it or not, there is nothing wrong with not having a boyfriend. You are not the only girl in the world who does not have a boyfriend. And finding a boyfriend just for the sake of being in a relationship is a bad idea. A healthy relationship can only happen when both people are ready and feel complete within themselves.

Sometimes when you focus too much attention on finding a boyfriend, you let your own dreams and interests slip away. And sometimes you even become depressed because you begin to base your happiness and sense of self-worth on whether or not you are in a relationship. Stop buying into the myth that you are not complete unless you're in a relationship.

In fact, one of the most obvious indicators of a confident and empowered girl is one who doesn't need a guy to validate her. Enjoy being single. Spend time doing things that interest you and contribute to your positive development. When the time is right you will find a boyfriend.

Power Move # 22

Be Smart About Dating

Two months ago you liked Darren. Then you liked James. Now you've got the biggest crush on Tommy. So many boys, so little time. At this stage in your life you are probably forming closer relationships with guys. Maybe you're going out on dates. Or perhaps you're seeing one guy exclusively. Whether you are casually dating or seeing one person pretty seriously, it's a good idea to be clear about the characteristics that you want in a boyfriend and know where you stand on important dating and relationship issues.

Here are some characteristics you might want to look for in a potential boyfriend.

- Someone who encourages you to pursue your goals and dreams.
- Someone who you can talk to about anything that is on your mind.
- Someone who makes you feel comfortable and emotionally supported.
- Someone who is on the right track.
- Someone who is kind and compassionate to others.
- Someone who shares his thoughts and feelings with you as well as listens to yours.
- Someone who is willing to meet your parents and who you are not ashamed of.
- Someone who has his own friends, but who is also willing to hang out with you and your friends.

- Someone who is willing to give you space.
- Someone who is consistent in his behavior.
- Someone who keeps his word.
- Someone who is honest and trustworthy.
- Someone who doesn't smoke, drink, use drugs or cut class.
- Someone who respects himself and others.

It's not enough to know what you want in a potential boyfriend, you also need to be clear about where you stand on important dating and relationship issues. You need to:

- Be clear about your values and what you will do when you're placed in situations that could compromise your values.
- Know what your boundaries are and how you are going to handle yourself if your potential boyfriend tries to push you to go too far.
- Let your parents meet him and take their opinions of him under serious consideration.
- Feel secure enough to speak up and stand up for yourself if your boyfriend does something that you don't agree with.
- Know the difference between a healthy relationship and an unhealthy one.
- Be honest about who you are, your beliefs and what you want out of the relationship.
- Find out about his values, likes, dislikes and goals to see if the two of you are headed in similar directions.
- Train yourself to be assertive so that you can stand up for yourself.
- Be comfortable with yourself, just as you are.
- Trust your instincts.

Power Move #23

Don't Hide Him From Your Parents

It can start with one little lie. You meet this cute guy. He asks you out. You say yes. But there's one little problem – you are not allowed to date yet. So what do you do? You tell your parents that you are going to the library with Lisa and you hook up with him behind their backs.

Or, let's say that you are allowed to date, but you get the feeling that your parents won't approve of him. So instead of introducing your new guy to your parents, you sneak around with him hoping that you don't get caught. The problems with these two scenarios are: First and foremost, you are putting yourself in a no-win situation. Whenever you start out with a lie, no matter how small, you have to keep on lying in order to keep the original lie from coming out. The more you lie, the worse you feel because eventually you will start to feel guilty about being so deceptive. And to tell you the truth it just takes too much energy to keep a lie going. Second, if your parents find out, they won't trust you anymore. If they don't trust you then they will be constantly on your back about every little thing you do. And this is no way to live.

Introducing a guy you like to your parents is not always easy because sometimes parents can say and do things that are embarrassing. Or, your boyfriend may say something stupid and confirm your parents' opinion of him. But the plus side is if you let your parents get to know him chances are they will feel more comfortable with your choices and they will start to trust you more. You will also put their minds at ease because they will know who you are spending time with. The biggest part of it all is if your parents know where you are and who you're with, they will be more inclined to loosen up their grip. Sounds like a win-win situation, right. So what are you waiting for? Stop hiding him and let your parents meet him.

Power Move #24

Heed The Warning Signs of An Abusive Relationship

When I was nineteen I used to go out with this guy who was physically abusive toward me. It didn't start out this way. In fact, in the beginning he acted like Prince Charming. He told me that I was beautiful and special. He wanted to spend all of his free time with me instead of hanging out with his friends. He brought me flowers, wrote me poetry, gave me expensive gifts and treated me like I was the most beautiful girl in the world. No guy had ever made me feel this way before. And after three months of being swept off my feet I was hooked. Then slowly things started to change.

He became extremely possessive and controlling. He started to comment on my clothes and if he didn't like what I was wearing he would tell me that I looked like a whore. If he saw me talking to another guy, he would accuse me of flirting. No matter what I did I always seemed to upset him. And little by little, my self-esteem and confidence started to fade away.

If he didn't like what I was wearing, I changed. If he didn't like one of my friends I stopped hanging out with them. After a while I stated to push my girlfriends aside. I even lied for him and made excuses for his behavior. Then one day he hit me. It wasn't a punch or a slap. He threw a sneaker at me. And since I didn't take it seriously, he went from sneaker throwing to slapping me around. I blamed myself because I thought that I should have known better. I couldn't understand how things got so out of hand. I was too embarrassed to tell anyone because I didn't want anyone to think that I was stupid or that I couldn't handle myself. But everyday that I stayed in that relationship a piece of me slipped away. Finally, I got out, but it wasn't easy.

In order to make sure that this doesn't happen to you, it is imperative that you learn how to recognize the warning signs of an unhealthy relationship. Following are some of the signs of an unhealthy relationship. If these signs ring true for the guy you are seeing, put some space between the two of you and talk to an adult.

- He comes on way too strong and wants to move a little too fast for you.
- He is extremely jealous.
- He tries to control what you wear, what you say and who you hang out with.
- He deals with his anger and conflicts by being aggressive or resorting to violence.
- He threatens or tries to intimidate you.
- He tries to pressure you to do things that make you feel uncomfortable.
- He is very moody, switching from being nice to getting loud and explosive.
- He tries to keep you all to himself away from your friends and family.
- He puts you down, hits, slaps or plays too rough with you.
- He compares you unfavorably with other girls and women.
- He uses alcohol and drugs and tries to get you to use.
- You feel like you have to walk on eggshells to stay on his good side.
- You feel like you have to pretend to be someone you're not in order to please him.
- You are not developing your own interests or participating in activities that contribute to your positive development.

- Your grades are slipping and you are not putting as much time and energy into your schoolwork.
- You have a "funny" feeling about him that keeps nagging at you.

These are some of the common signs of a potentially abusive partner and an unhealthy relationship. Pay attention to them and above all else trust your instincts. And remember in a healthy relationship you will feel safe, empowered and respected.

Power Move #25

Watch Out for Older Guys

It's only natural to feel flattered when an older guy gives you a compliment or shows interest in you. It is also not that uncommon for girls to date guys who are a year or two older. But when you date a guy who is much older than you, there are many dangerous risks involved. For starters, because he has more life experience than you and is probably already sexually active, he will know just what to say and do to initiate a sexual relationship with you or get you to do things that you normally would not do. And the funny thing is because he is so experienced at this, you may not even feel like you've been manipulated.

I know. I know what you're thinking: *I'm smart, mature and I can handle an older guy.* It may seem that way. And if he's very experienced in initiating relationships with underage girls, he may even tell you that you're mature for your age and he normally doesn't go for younger girls. But no matter what he tells you or how mature you think you are, you may not be able to comfortably handle everything an older guy throws your way.

Sometimes older guys go after much younger girls because they believe that it will be easier to manipulate and control them. They know that you're still growing and developing and you haven't had as much experience dealing with different situations as women their own age do. They also know that you won't be as able as a woman their own age to see past their lies and lines.

Perhaps that older guy who likes you is really a nice guy who just happens to be romantically interested in you. But just think about this: If he is

49

such a decent guy, why would he overstep the appropriate boundaries by pursuing a romantic and possibly sexual relationship with an underage girl? It just makes sense that if a guy is looking for a healthy relationship based on equality, shared values and common interests he would find someone his own age.

It might be flattering to go out with an older guy, but it's not worth the risks. Here are some of the risks involved in having a relationship with a much older guy. You may:

- Start lying to your parents, because you know that they won't approve.
- Try to act older than your age to prove how mature you are.
- Stop doing things that are normal for girls your age.
- Get your friends involved in deception by asking them to cover for you while you are out with him.
- Feel pressured to have sex or go farther than you want to go because chances are that he's already sexually active.
- Become exposed to a sexually transmitted disease because he is more likely to have had other sexual experiences.
- Be expected to do things that are not appropriate for your age or level of development.
- Go against your values or beliefs in order to please him.

If an older guy is coming on to you tell your parents, a teacher or another adult you trust. In the United States it is illegal for an adult to have sex with a minor even if the minor wants to. Although an older guy may make you feel special, if he truly believes that you are special then he will not cross the line with you. It's that simple.

Power Move #26

Don't Ditch Your Girlfriends For A Guy

There is one thing about a lot of girls and women that drives me absolutely crazy. They ditch their girlfriends as soon as they get involved with a guy. You know the type: the girlfriend who makes plans with you then changes those plans if her new guy wants to spend time with her. Here's the scenario: You and your girlfriend made plans to go to the movies on Friday. You're all revved up. Just when you're about to walk out the door, you get a phone call that sounds something like this, *Hey girl, I hope you don't mind but David called and he really wants to get together tonight. I told him that I had plans with you but that I would give you a call to see if you still wanted to go. Besides I heard that the movie we're supposed to go see isn't really that good anyway.*

You tell her that you don't mind if she goes out with David, but deep inside you're disappointed. Nurturing healthy relationships with your girlfriends is just as important, if not more so, as nurturing healthy relationships with potential boyfriends. When you push your girlfriends aside for a guy, what you're really saying is, " I don't value your friendship as much as I value guys." Girls seem to put their friends on the backburner in order to hook up with a guy. This is not fair and if you make a habit of it then you are not being a good friend. Show your friends that you value them by making time for them and not backing out of your plans when a more appealing offer comes along.

Boys will come and go, but good friendships will last a long, long time.

Power Move #27

Don't Get Involved With Guys Headed Down The Wrong Path

Just about every girl at some point in her dating life may fall for a guy who is headed down the wrong path. You know the type: defiant, a rebel and definitely not the kind of guy that your parents would approve of. This is the guy who more often than not acts like a complete jerk yet all the girls seem to secretly like him.

The reasons so many girls like bad boys are; the excitement, the challenge and the thrill of being able to brag to all of your friends how you were the one who was able to capture his heart. But what you need to keep in mind is, what starts out as an exciting adventure almost always turns into grief and drama.

Growing up I always thought of myself as a smart girl, but more often than not I got involved with guys who were headed down the wrong path. At the time I thought I was being cool and adventurous but in reality my choices put me in some pretty risky situations.

Sometimes we get so caught up in wanting to rebel against our parents, fit in with the popular crowd or feel powerful that we get involved with people who are no good for us. A guy who is on the wrong path can indirectly take you off your path. If he's cutting class, smoking, drinking or getting high, you may find yourself doing these things also, just to keep up with him. And the truth is any guy who is worth it will not only be on the right track, he will also bring out your best qualities. If a guy cannot positively contribute to your life, then he should not be in it.

Power Move #28

Leave Her Boyfriend Alone

Some girls get a kick out of going after another girl's boyfriend. They think that if they can pull a guy away from another girl that it somehow makes them smarter and more powerful than the other girl. Well, guess what? It doesn't. What it makes you is a backstabber. This is not to say that the guy is not a fault for stepping out on the other girl. He is. But what is also important is that girls honor the code of sisterhood by looking out for one another and not back biting each other.

More and more, it seems like girls are in constant competition with each other trying to out do one another. You don't have to buy into this negative behavior. You are too smart for that. When you intentionally go after another girl's boyfriend or set out to sabotage another girl, you are not only hurting her, you are also hurting yourself. How so? You cut yourself off from other girls who if given the opportunity could be good friends to you. And if you gain a reputation for being a backstabber, no one will want to have anything to do with you.

You may think that being kind to other girls is not important, but it is. It expands your circle of friends and builds your reputation as a stand up kind of girl. Sure, you are not going to like every girl you meet, but that does not mean that you have to gear up for combat or deliberately try to hurt other girls either. Respect yourself by respecting other girls and expand your social circle by honoring the code of sisterhood. You never know when you are going to need another girl to respect you.

Power Move #29

Trust You'll Bounce Back From A Break-up

Back when I was in high school one of my girlfriends had a sleep over. Everyone was laughing and having a good time, but I just didn't feel like laughing. My boyfriend and I had just broken up and I was devastated. Then "our song" came on the radio and I started to cry. I felt like my world was crashing down all around me.

Sometimes a break-up can leave you feeling this way and it seems like the pain will never end. But eventually it will. You can help yourself bounce back by doing three things: letting your feelings out, talking with people you trust and keeping yourself busy.

1Let Your Feelings Out

After a break-up you will probably experience many different emotions in a short period of time. One minute you'll be waiting by the phone hoping that he calls to say how sorry he is, the next moment you'll completely and utterly hate his guts. Don't try to hide your feelings. If you need to cry, cry. If you want to yell in the privacy of your room, yell. If you want to write in a journal or make up a song or poem about it, go ahead. The important thing is that you let your feelings out in a healthy way.

2. Talk With Someone You Trust

Sometimes when you are going through a difficult situation the best thing that you can do to feel better is to talk about your experiences and feelings. Painful feelings can seem overwhelming and when you keep the pain to yourself it can become very intense.

Talk to your parents, a counselor, a teacher or your best friend. Just talk.

Chances are they've been through a similar experience and will understand exactly what you are going through.

3. Keep Yourself Busy

The worst thing that you can do if you're trying to get over a break-up is to sit around the house moping all day. Keep yourself busy. Go visit a friend. Volunteer for a good cause. Sign up for a workshop. It really doesn't matter what you choose to do as long as you focus your time and attention on something other than the break-up. While keeping busy won't make you completely forget about your ex, it will help you to see that you have what it takes to move on. Use this time to reconnect with friends and family, take up a hobby or help someone else who is worse off than you. And sooner than you know it, you'll be back to your old self again.

Power Move #30

Try Not to Get Stressed Out By Cliques

Junior high school is probably the place where you will first notice that most of the kids group together in cliques. Like clubs, cliques tend to form around people who share similar interests or who have something in common. The problem with cliques is they can really stress a girl out. Because instead of focusing your attention on doing well in school and exploring cool things that interest you, you'll be worried about who's in the clique and who's out. When you are part of a clique you tend to be restricted to a particular group. And if you want to hang out with someone who is not part of the clique the rest of the group may give you a hard time or stop hanging out with you all together.

Being popular and hanging out with the coolest kids might be important to you, but also strive to make your own friends outside of the group. Don't forget to be kind to the unpopular girls. Join activities and clubs because you are interested in them, not because your friends want you to join. Cultivate your own interests and think for yourself.

I know that you are at a stage in your life where fitting in is important, but try not to stress yourself out over it. True friends will accept you and stand by your side even if you do something that is different from the rest of the crowd. While cliques can be cool, they usually don't stick around during the tough times.

Power Move #31

Don't Use Friendship As A Weapon

Your best friend Kelly told you that if you hang out with Crystal she would stop speaking to you. Nikki told you if you were really Kelly's friend, you wouldn't be hanging out with Crystal in the first place. These are just two examples of how friendship can be used as a weapon. It's not nice or fair to try to manipulate your friends by using your friendship to coerce them or make them feel guilty. This is called relational aggression. A lot of girls have a tendency to use friendship as a weapon. It starts with a whisper followed by a sinister giggle or dirty look. And without one friend saying a word to the other, they both know that the tension is on.

The golden rule to live by is; treat your friends the way you want to be treated. If you don't want your friends to use their friendship with you as a weapon, then make sure that you do not use friendship as a weapon with others. This takes practice, but if you make a conscious effort not to manipulate your friends or allow them to manipulate you, you'll develop stronger and healthier friendships.

Power Move #32

Be Careful Not to Let Your Friends Do Your Thinking for You

Have you ever changed your opinion about something in order to fit in with your friends? How about gossiped about a classmate just because the rest of your friends didn't like her? Lied about something you did so the other girls would be more accepting of you? Maybe they'll let you in their clique, but then what? Friendships are not true friendships if you cannot be yourself and express your opinions freely. No friend or group is worth the trouble it takes of having to change your personality or values to fit in.

The funny thing about cliques is that alliances can change at the drop of a hat. Today you and Ramona are friends. Next week the two of you are barely speaking and you don't even know why. Last week you and Jessica were gossiping about Toya. This week you and Toya are trashing Jessica's new outfit.

The temptation to let your friends set your standards can be overwhelming, but you can make up your own mind and decide to do what feels right for you. You may not think that changing your personality to fit in with your peers is that big of a deal, but it is. Because whenever you change your mind as a result of someone else's influence you are not being true to yourself. And that makes you a follower.

Today, make the decision to be your own person, follow your own lead and stand firm in your own decisions.

Power Move # 33

Know That Rainy Days Won't Last Forever

You tried out for the cheerleading squad and didn't make the cut. The new guy you like has a crush on your best friend. You didn't ace that important exam you've been cramming for. You get the gist: A situation did not work out the way you hoped and you're feeling a little down.

You've probably heard the saying, " Rainy days won't last forever." Believe it or not, this saying is really true. Everyone goes through bad experiences, this just happens to be your bad experience. The good news is it's not the end of the world. It may seem like it, but it is not. Try to focus your attention on what you can learn from this experience and remember that better days lie ahead.

The quickest way to recover from a bad experience is to develop the attitude that every setback or challenge is an opportunity to grow as well as develop an underdeveloped characteristic like: faith, patience, determination or courage. Take stock of all the positive things that you have to offer and open your eyes to all the good things that exist in your life like: your health, your youth, people who care about you and a Creator who loves you more than you'll ever know.

Life isn't perfect, but if you take stock of all the ways that you are blessed, you will see that life is good.

Power Move # 34

Learn to Say No

It's a week before finals. You planned to go straight home after school so that you can get some extra study time in. Just as you close your locker one of your friends catches up with you and asks you to go to the mall. You say yes, but you really want to go home and study. Or you're at the movies with a guy you really like. He kisses you and starts going further than you are comfortable with, instead of telling him that he's moving too fast, you say nothing hoping he'll stop.

When these kinds of situations happen to you, the most powerful thing that you can do is exercise your right to say "no." Saying no can be difficult because you might find yourself wondering how the other person is going to take it. But what you need to keep in mind is when someone makes an imposition on you or crosses the line they could care less about how you are going to take it. If they truly cared then they would not have made the unfair request or crossed the line with you in the first place.

When you put your feelings on the back burner to please others you are being unfair to yourself because you are neglecting your own needs. The next time you find yourself in a situation where you feel pressured to go along with something that you really don't want to do, take 60 seconds to think through the situation then say no. Stand firm in your decision. Saying no is not about hurting others, it's about developing the assertiveness skills to set boundaries and stand by your decisions. With practice it gets easier. While it's nice to think about others, it is also perfectly ok to put yourself first.

Power Move #35

Don't Take Everything So Personally

A surefire way to create a ton of unnecessary stress for yourself is to take everything personally. You've probably known people who make a big deal out of every situation, big or small. The kind of people who get bent out of shape easily and gear up for battle every time they can't have their way making it impossible to get along with them or even sit in the same room. You may even find yourself watching everything you say and do or avoiding them all together just so you don't have to deal with their constant complaining and bickering.

The problem with taking things too personally is twofold: First, it is extremely stressful. Second, people will start to pull away from you because no one wants to be around someone who complains and nitpicks all day.

What's interesting is when you really think about it, you will come to find that it takes too much energy to get bent out of shape over every little thing. You could put that energy to better use by focusing on your schoolwork, hanging out with your friends or developing your interests. Everything is not about you so try not to take things so personally.

Power Move #36

Look Inside Yourself for Happiness

Some people look for happiness in the strangest places. They believe that if they have lots of clothes, money, look like the images portrayed in the media and are in a relationship with someone who is cute and popular that they will be happy. But this is not true because happiness comes from within. Happiness does not come from what you have. It comes from who you are on the inside and the relationships you nurture with loved ones.

There are many attractive people with money and a fabulous wardrobe who are miserable. Why? Because external things can't sustain true happiness and they can't give you peace of mind. I'll bet that you either know or have seen people on television who on the outside appeared to have everything going for them but still don't seem happy. The biggest mistake that you can ever make is to look to material things to make you happy. If you do, you will never be satisfied.

True happiness comes from loving yourself, pursuing your dreams, developing a grateful heart and spending time with people who care about you. Today, write down ten things that you are grateful for and look inside yourself for happiness.

Power Move #37

Express Yourself

I'll bet that there have been times that you were upset with someone and when they asked you what was wrong, you said; "nothing" and gave them the cold shoulder. Even though you were probably fuming inside and the other person could see that you were visibly upset, I'll bet that you denied that there was anything wrong. When you don't express your feelings and you allow negative feelings to fester, you hurt yourself because your negative feelings will get the best of you. When this happens you become bitter and resentful and sometimes even physically ill.

Instead of giving someone the cold shoulder try expressing your feelings calmly and honestly. If you are upset because your best friend backed out of previous plans with you to hang out with someone else, tell her. If you are upset that your boyfriend behaved like a jerk in front of his friends, tell him. The important thing here is to get into the habit of respectfully telling people how you feel. Using the silent treatment will not resolve the issue. Besides the other person might not even know why you're upset with them. Express yourself so that you can resolve the issue and move forward.

Power Move # 38

Trust Your Intuition

There is an old saying that goes, "believe none of what you hear, half of what you see and all of what you feel." In many instances, this saying is true. As a teen I remember having a girlfriend whose uncle made me feel uncomfortable. He was very friendly and everybody liked him, but something inside of me told me to be careful around him. I couldn't put my finger on it, but I knew in my gut not to trust him. The funny thing was I had another girlfriend who felt the exact same way but she did not listen to her intuition. And a couple of weeks later she told me that he tried to get her to have sex with him.

As humans, especially females we are equipped with a virtually fool proof guidance system called intuition. This guidance system lets us know when to trust and when to keep our guards up, when to move forward on something and when to wait. Intuition is a powerful tool that you can learn to use with practice and focused attention. The more you listen to that voice inside your head that warns you of possible danger, the better able you will be to read the signs that your intuition sends you to keep you safe.

Try to pay attention to the signals that your mind and body send you throughout the day. Do you feel uneasy around a certain person or queasy in your stomach when you think about a particular situation? Be aware of the signs that your intuition sends you and if you learn to trust that tiny voice inside your head, you'll rarely go wrong.

Power Move #39

When You Don't Know What Else To Do Pray

Prayer is one of the most powerful tools that you will ever have at your disposal. So when you feel like you are at your wits end and you don't know what else to do, pray. When life feels bad and your situation seems to be spinning out of control the smartest thing that you can do is pray. Prayer really does change things. If it doesn't change the situation, it will change your outlook and give you the strength to get through it.

The wonderful thing about prayer is that there is no single set way to pray. You can pray kneeling, standing, sitting down or lying down. You can pray any time of the day. You don't even have to think of a bunch of fancy words to say, just tell God what you're feeling and going through. If you don't know where to start, start by asking for God's grace and mercy. Ask God to fill your heart and mind with peace and goodness. Pray for guidance, wisdom, strength and courage. Pray for people who are worse off than you. Even pray for people you don't like. They probably need it the most.

You may not see any tangible benefits right away. You may not even understand why you are going through whatever it is that you are going through, but if you keep the faith and turn your troubles over to God, things will eventually work out for your greater good.

Power Move #40

Keep A Journal

I have kept a journal since high school. When I look back at what I wrote, I think it's pretty amazing to see how much I have experienced, learned and grown. I have written about my dreams, plans desires, family, friends and boyfriends. Sometimes I look back and laugh. Sometimes I cry. Keeping a journal is a good way to keep your plans and dreams alive. It is also extremely therapeutic.

The wonderful thing about keeping a journal is it belongs to you and you can write about whatever you want to write about. I have even written down songs and poems that I've made up over the years. You can decorate your journal with glitter, beautiful fabric, pictures from magazines or anything else that you can think of.

Cherish the special moments in your life and privately talk about the not so great moments by keeping a journal. When you look back on your life, you will come to appreciate the joys, dreams and struggles that you captured in your journal.

Power Move #41

Make The World A Better Place To Live

Making the world a better place to live is not as difficult as you might think. It starts by simply deciding to do one small thing to make someone else's life a little better like: visiting someone in the hospital, donating clothes or canned goods to a homeless shelter, helping your teacher after class, standing up for someone who is unable to stand up for themselves, advocating for a cause you strongly believe in or anything else that you can think of that would positively impact others.

There are lots of girls your age who are involved in really cool projects and giving back to humanity in some very interesting ways. You can log on to *www.teenvoices.com* or *www.unitedway.org* to get ideas about ways that you can get involved and give back.

It takes all of us to make the world a better place to live. Make today your day to give back. There is always something that you can do. Why not get together with some of your classmates and sponsor a contest in your school aimed at giving back to the community. When you give to others you get back so much more in return.

Power Move #42

If A Friend's In Serious Trouble Get Help

One of the hardest things that you may ever have to do for a friend who you suspect is dealing with a very serious issue is break the friendship code of secrecy by telling an adult. If you have a friend who is dealing with a really big issue like: a drug or alcohol problem, an abusive relationship, thoughts of suicide or anything else that could place her in serious jeopardy, the best thing that you can do for her is to go to an adult for help. Talk to your school counselor, your parents or any adult that you trust to get their perspective on the problem. The good thing about sharing the situation with an adult is you get someone with more life experience and resources who can help you and your friend figure out what to do.

Initially, your friend may be angry that you told someone else about her issue. She may even accuse you of betraying her confidence. But if you truly care about her, then it's only right that you would take positive action to get her the help that she needs. Even if she thinks that she can handle the situation by herself, there are some problems that are just too big for people to handle alone. If nothing else you can get advice on how to best help your friend. You don't even have to tell the adult who your friend is, just explain the situation and ask for his or her guidance.

It can be difficult to break a friend's confidence, but if you are worried about her safety or well-being tell someone else. You might think that keeping things quiet is the best way to show her that you care, but in the long run keeping a serious problem a secret may do more harm than good.

Power Move #43

Cultivate Your Interests

As a little girl I was often asked: *What do you want to be when you grow up?* And my answer to this question changed as often as my interests did. At one time I daydreamed about being a famous singer and songwriter. I would make up songs as well as participate in talent shows and plays. Then I wanted to be a television news reporter. I took classes in media broadcasting and studied different TV reporters. I even read their biographies. I imagined being like Barbara Walters or Connie Chung keeping citizens abreast of the latest happenings around the world.

After graduating college I became interested in public speaking and writing and discovered that I had a knack for it. I read books on these subjects and took classes to improve my skills. And several years later I started my own company where I travel across the country giving business seminars and motivational talks. At this writing I am also the author of five self-published books. I am doing what I love and earning a living at the same time. This is the payoff I received from cultivating my interests. Things are not always easy. As an owner of a small business I have my ups and downs. I have to be really diligent about managing my time and money. But no matter how tough things get, I wouldn't trade my lifestyle for anything. And the same thing can happen for you if you start to cultivate your interests.

Whatever your interests are, take time to develop them. Take classes. Read books. Be proactive about learning as much as you can about the things that interest you. We live in a culture where success is often associated with material possessions and other external things. I would like to offer you a broader definition of success: being happy with yourself and doing what you love. I believe that if you take the time to cultivate your interests then apply yourself, you can have the best of both worlds, a career that fulfills your sense of purpose as well as financial stability.

Power Move #44

Don't Place Limitations On Yourself

There's on old story about a flea circus that was known all over the world for their ability to jump extremely high. The flea trainer used to train the fleas by putting them in a glass jar to see how far they could jump. The fleas would jump all the way to the top of the jar, hit the lid and come back down. The flea trainer continued to train the fleas this way until he noticed something very strange: even when he removed the lid from the jar the fleas would not jump out. Not because they didn't have the ability to jump higher, but because they believed that lid was still there.

Many people condition themselves to believe that they cannot go any higher than the limitations that other people have placed on them or that they have placed on themselves. It's like being in a glass jar with an imaginary lid preventing them from pursuing their goals and dreams. So they go through life never realizing their full potential and putting up mental roadblocks that set them up to fail before they even try. This is no way to go through life. Sure you'll encounter obstacles and there will even be people who will not believe in you but you cannot allow obstacles or short-sighted people to prevent you from going after all that you were meant to have and become.

You have what it takes to succeed. And if you follow your dreams with persistence, patience and focus you will accomplish whatever it is that you set out to do. Free your mind from limited thinking. Instead of thinking about all the reasons why you cannot succeed or the obstacles that are stacked

71

against you, focus your attention on all the reasons why you can succeed and all that you already have going for you. Make the decision to overcome obstacles by removing your lid from the glass jar.

Power Move #45

Earn Your Own Money

What do you do on the weekends and during summer vacation? Have you ever thought about getting a job? By this point in your life, you are well aware of the fact that money doesn't grow on trees. I'll bet that being privy to this well-known bit of information probably doesn't stop you from asking your parents for money so that you can buy that new CD or that cute little outfit you saw at the mall. However, sometimes your parents need you to give them a financial break. At times they will have to say no to you because they have other financial obligations like: groceries, rent, a mortgage, car payments and other expenses that you cannot even begin to imagine. But if you had your own money, you wouldn't have to depend on your parents for all the little extras that you like.

There are endless ways that you can earn your own money. During the summer you can work as a camp counselor, office assistant or maintenance assistant. You could work at a bookstore, gift shop, clothing store or fast food restaurant. You can baby-sit, house-sit, pet-sit, walk dogs, wash cars, mow lawns, shovel snow, tutor, offer your typing services, bake cookies or set-up a lemonade stand.

The key to getting a job is to find out who needs help and offer your services. Think out of the box and be creative. Today, keep your mind open to ideas about things that you can do to earn your own money.

Power Move #46

Be A Penny Pincher

In the previous power move we talked about earning your own money. This is the first step. Once you start to earn your own money the next step is to make sure that you save a little. It's a good idea to create a plan on how you will spend and save your money. In my other book, *Young, Gifted and Doing It*, power moves 21 through 23 offer step-by-step tips for managing money, but in this book I want to highlight the importance of being frugal. You are never too young to start saving money. Whether you open up a savings account or put your money in a piggy bank, the key here is to save a set amount each time you receive income. Why not put half of the money in the bank and spend the other half on things you like, like: clothes, hanging out with friends and other things that you enjoy.

When I was twelve I used to have a piggy bank where I kept all of my change. When the piggy bank was full my mom took me to the bank and we exchanged the change for dollars. The change added up and I was able to buy a lot of cool stuff. But no matter how much money I got, I always put a little away. This strategy gave me financial freedom at a young age.

Start pinching your pennies and watch your money grow. It may be fun to spend money, but it's even more fun when you have some left over for a rainy day.

Power Move #47

Let Go Of The Need To Be Perfect

A huge, sometimes overwhelming source of stress for girls, especially teenage ones is the need for everything and everyone to be perfect. Whether it's your weight, hair, a facial feature, a school project gone awry or a situation that didn't work out the way you planned, striving for perfection will drive you nuts. Why? Because nobody's perfect. Not even you. And no matter how hard you try you cannot guarantee that every situation will work out exactly the way you plan down to the last detail. Instead of striving for perfection, strive for excellence. Put your best effort forth in all that you do. And no matter how things work out, if in your heart of hearts you know that you did your best, let it go and move on.

The need for perfection will make you an obsessive and compulsive person. And no one will want to hang around you because your perfectionism will make it too much work to remain friends with you. What I have found to be more realistic is to develop an attitude of excellence by doing your absolute best. And if the situation doesn't work out the way you planned, learn from your mistakes.

Over and over, I hear girls say things like: *If only I looked like so and so. If only I was smarter. If only I was thin.* This kind of thinking guarantees a life of frustration, because you will go through life picking yourself and everyone else apart. I even hear some people say things like, *"I am not hard to please, I just have exceptionally high standards."* High standards are good, but sometimes we use impossible standards as a way to mask our own insecurities and avoid doing the self-work that is necessary for living a happy and purposeful life.

Learn to experience the blessing in imperfection while always striving to do your best. Be less obsessive about what you perceive to be your weaknesses and put your energy into maximizing your strengths. As you let go of the need to be perfect, you will enjoy the benefits of a happier and less stressed life.

Power Move #48

Make Room for New Friends

Kimberly is your best friend. She has a new friend Veronica. You don't like Veronica. Kimberly invites Veronica to tag along with the two of you wherever you go. Kimberly also invited Veronica to your spa night when it was just supposed to be the two of you. Veronica irritates the heck out of you and you don't know how much longer you'll be able to take her.

Before you say or do something that you can't take back, ask yourself: *Do I really dislike Veronica or am I a little jealous because she's spending so much time with my best friend?* Whether you just don't like Veronica or you're upset because you feel like she is intruding on your friendship, you are going to have to try to get along with her if you do not want to place Kimberly in an awkward situation. Moving from a duo to a crowded trio can be a drag, but it is also an opportunity to make a new friend. Rather than compete for Kimberly's friendship or complain about Veronica, why not get to know Veronica for yourself and see if you can build your own friendship. Who knows? You might be pleasantly surprised.

The worst thing that you can do to a friend is to make her feel like she has to choose sides. More often than not, instead of getting her undying loyalty, she will distance herself from you. Express your feelings without trashing the other person. You can tell your friend that you don't mind hanging out as a trio but sometimes you'd like it to be just the two of you. If you really put your mind to it, I'll bet that you will find that you have room in your heart for another friend.

Power Move #49

Try Something New

Have you ever tried something new only to be pleasantly surprised by how much you enjoyed yourself? Discovering new things about yourself makes your life rich. The more you try out different hobbies and activities, the more you expand your horizons. The more you expand your horizons the more interesting you become as a person.

On Saturday mornings, I often watch the cooking shows and daydream about making elaborate and exotic meals. This peaked my interest in cooking. As a result I signed up for a cooking class and discovered that cooking was therapeutic for me. The smell of the different spices and the anticipation of eating a fabulous meal filled my heart with delight. I also found that I enjoy cooking for friends and family because it's just one more way that I express myself.

Today, think about something that peaks your interest and go for it. Try different things until you discover what truly brings you joy. Take a dance class, guitar lessons, make up songs, write a poem, go sailing or rock climbing, trace your family history, go to a museum. When you try new things you open yourself up to limitless possibilities.

Power Move #50

Follow Your Dreams

Just for today, imagine that there were no obstacles or restrictions to hold you back. What would you do? Would you plan that trip to France that you've always dreamed about? Would you audition for the school play? Would you recite a poem at an open mike reading? Submit your essay in a writing contest? Well, today is your day to go for it. You can do anything that you set your mind to because you have talents and abilities that you haven't even begun to tap.

Picture yourself winning the essay contest, or getting a thunderous applause for your poem, having the audience give you a standing ovation as you make your acting debut or dining at a little French Café in the heart of Paris. Talk about your plans and dreams. Write about them. Then, take one small step to make them come true.

Your imagination is a powerhouse of endless possibilities. It can be used to create the kind of life the most people only dream of. It will help you to anticipate obstacles and prepare yourself for them. Hold a mental picture in your mind's eye of you succeeding at achieving your goals. Picture yourself vividly accomplishing one small task at a time. This may seem a little silly at first and some people may even laugh at you because they just don't get it. But the surest way to turn a dream into a plan is to picture it then work out the steps that are necessary to move your idea into action. When Walt Disney drew a picture of a mouse and presented his ideas to a corporate board they all laughed at him, including his own brother. But he kept thinking about his dream, talking about his dream and making calculated steps to move it from a fantasy in his head into a tangible reality and you know how the story ends: It ended with the creation of Disney World. Guess who had the last laugh?

If there is something that you've been dying to do or a dream that you've been secretly holding on to, now is the time to go for it. Get out of your comfort zone and blaze your own trail. Who knows? You just might succeed.

Power Move #51

Learn From Your Sheroes

Learning from your favorite sheroes is one of the smartest strategies that you can put into practice. Why? Because you can learn about what they did when they were your age and throughout their lives that enabled them to get where they are today.

As a teen girl of this generation you are fortunate enough to have examples all around you of positive, powerful women who are doing some pretty amazing things. From doctors and lawyers to small business owners and CEO's of large corporations to educators, activists and stay-at-home moms, there are examples of sheroes wherever you look.

Some of my favorite sheroes are Oprah Winfrey, Hillary Clinton and Maya Angelou. I try to learn as much as I can about these women and the steps they took to pursue their passions so that I can apply some of the same principles in my own life.

You can start learning from your favorite sheroes by: visiting the library, reading up on great women in history, watching documentaries, going online or shadowing and volunteering for a woman you admire so that you can get a clearer picture of what her profession entails. Talk to women who are doing what you would like to do or what you find interesting. Don't just ask about their career but also about personal struggles and mistakes they've made along the way.

Come up with a plan for connecting with your sheroes. Find out from your school or local community center if there are mentoring or internship programs that you could apply for. Remember that every successful woman was your age once, with the same pressures and insecurities as you. There's no reason why you can't prepare yourself today to be someone else's future sheroe.

Power Move #52

Remember That Life Is A Journey

Life is a journey. It is a never-ending quest to learn, share and grow. Just a few years ago you were a little girl and now you are a blossoming young woman changing, growing and learning. Celebrate yourself. Appreciate your special qualities. Love yourself completely. Know that in life you will have good times and bad times and the bad times won't last forever. You are smart, strong and resilient. And you will make it.

Every once in awhile do a periodic self-check and ask yourself: *Who am I? Where am I headed? Why am I here? What do I want? What am I good at? What do I need to work on? What can I contribute to humanity?*

As you uncover the answers to these questions you will come to know yourself more. You will develop a clearer picture about the direction that you are headed in. Be thoughtful and reflective as you discover the wonderful and dynamic person you are meant to be.

Know that you are just as amazing as everyone around you and that there are people who think you're pretty, smart, fun to be around and good hearted. Know that there are so many wonderful things about you and if you focus on your strengths you will come to appreciate yourself for the **Cool, Confident and Strong** young woman that you are.

Closing Words

The closer you get to adulthood, the more complicated life gets. It can be difficult to make sense of all your feelings and experiences. It is my hope that **Cool, Confident and Strong** empowers you with practical advice that you can apply to the many new and sometimes challenging situations that you will face as a growing young woman. Know that you are special and always, always, always be true to yourself.

Please drop me an e-mail message at: *teenpowermove@aol.com* to let me know what you thought about **Cool, Confident and Strong**. Make sure to write the phrase "Cool, Confident and Strong" in the subject message area so that I will know that you are writing in response to this book. Thanks.

Discussion Guide

One of the most empowering things that you can do for an adolescent girl is to initiate a discussion around the issues that impact today's teenage girls like: identity, self-esteem, dating and relationships, friendships, relational aggression and the increased challenges that she faces at school and at home. Many of these issues are presented in **Cool, Confident and Strong.**

If you open the door to honest communication you will find that she will come to you about anything that is on her mind. She will also come to you for advice on issues that are important to her. And isn't that what she really needs: A caring adult who she can count on for guidance and sound advice?

The discussion questions in this book are designed for you to use with your daughter if you are a parent or if you are a youth service provider with your girls group. You may even want to think about starting your very own *Cool, Confident and Strong* group. Before you use the discussion questions, read the book thoroughly, reflect on the issues presented then get together with a group of mothers and daughters or if you're a youth service provider, your girls group and initiate a discussion around the questions that I have provided in this section.

It helps to ask the questions in a group setting and in the third person because this allows the girls to answer the questions honestly without fear of judgment or reprisal.

1. In Power Move #1 *Love Yourself Just The Way You Are,* the author says: "that there is no such thing as the perfect kind of beauty, because we are all beautiful in our own unique way." Do you think that there is a great deal of pressure for girls your age to fit a certain ideal? How does this kind of pressure affect the self-esteem in teenage girls as well as the kinds of decisions they make? What kinds of things have you heard or seen girls do to themselves and each other as a result of this pressure?

2. When girls want to be popular, what kinds of things do they do? Are some girls willing to go too far to be popular? What do you consider going too far? Do some girls change their personality to be popular? Could you give an example? Are girls ever mean to the unpopular girls? Why do you think this is so? In Power Move #30 *Try Not to Get Stressed Out By Cliques,* the author says to be kind to girls who are not part of your clique. It this easier said then done? Explain how.

3. Is it important to have high self-esteem? Why or why not? How can you tell if a person has high self-esteem? What about low self-esteem? Can a person be popular, cute, have nice clothes and still have low self-esteem? In *Cool, Confident and Strong*

the author provides girls with a five step plan for building high self-esteem which includes: positive self-talk, surrounding yourself with positive people, reminding yourself that you have what it takes to go far, participating in activities that you enjoy and putting your best foot forward. Besides these strategies, what other kinds of things can girls do to feel confident and good about themselves.

4. In Power Move #7 *Look Hot Without Taking Off Your Clothes,* the author says that we live in a culture where dressing scantily and provocatively seems to be the new norm. Do you think that some girls look and act too old for their age and dress too revealing? Why do you think that some girls dress this way? Are there any risks or dangers that can come with dressing too provocatively? Is there a difference between looking trendy and looking trashy? Give some examples.

5. Do girls compete with each other? Do they trust each other? Do you personally know anyone who has ever been betrayed by someone who she considered a friend? What happened? In Power Move #14 *Put An End To Petty Jealousy,* the author says instead of competing with other girls discover what your special qualities are and participate in activities that make you happy. Besides these two strategies is there anything else that you can think of that

might help girls not to be so competitive with each other?

6. Peer pressure can get the best of even the most strong-willed teen. How powerful is peer pressure in your school and in your social circle? What kinds of things are girls pressured to do? How do they handle it? Why are some girls better are handling negative peer pressure than others? In *Cool, Confident and Strong* the author suggests that teens go through common peer pressure situations with their parents in order to come up with strategies for handling difficult situations. Do you think this strategy can be helpful? Why or why not? If not, what else can teens do to develop skills for handling negative pressure from their peers?

7. In Power Move #18 *Choose Your Friends Wisely*, the author reminds us that pulling away from a friend is not easy but once in a while it might be necessary. How would you know when it's time to pull away from a friend? What are the signs of an unhealthy friendship? What about a healthy one? What is the best way to end a friendship if the two friends don't get along any more or are headed in different directions? What qualities are important in a friendship? What should a true friend never do?

8. Today's teenage girls are bombarded with sex. You see it on television and in the

movies. You hear about it on the radio and read about it in magazines. It's a subject that teens talk about in the cafeteria, in the halls and sometimes in class. In Power Move # 20 *Don't Get Suckered Into Sex,* the author stresses the benefits of waiting. Do you think that girls your age are pressured to have sex? What kinds of sexual pressures do girls your age face? Why do some girls choose to have sex? Why do some wait? Can you be a virgin and still be popular? When is the most appropriate time to have sex: at age eighteen, when you're in a long-term relationship or after marriage? What are some of the benefits of waiting? What are some of the consequences of engaging in sex too early? There are so many mixed messages out there concerning sex. If you move too fast you're considered loose. If you put sex on hold, sometimes you're considered a prude. Is it better to be loose or considered a prude? What other words can you use to add a more positive spin on making the choice to wait?

9. In Power Move # 22 *Be Smart About Dating,* the author talks about the importance of knowing where you stand on important dating and relationship issues as well as knowing what qualities are important to you in a potential boyfriend, why do you think that these are important strategies? What's important to girls your age in a potential boyfriend? What qualities should

he have? What kinds of behavior should girls stay away from?

10.   In Power Move #23 *Don't Hide Him From Your Parents*, the author stresses the importance of introducing a guy you're interested in to your parents. What are some of the benefits of introducing a guy you like to your parents? Why do some girls hide their boyfriends from their parents? What can parents do to get their daughters to become more open with them about their dating and relationship choices?

11.   In Power Move # 24 *Heed the Warning Signs of An Abusive Relationship,* the author identifies some of the warning signs of an abusive relationship. Why is it important for girls your age to know the facts about teen dating violence? Why do some girls stay with guys who abuse them? Does teen dating violence occur in your school? Is there someone that teens can talk to in your school or community center if they are in an abusive relationship or suspect that their boyfriend has the potential to become abusive?

12.   Sometimes older guys try to get junior high and high school girls to go out with them. In Power Move #25 *Watch Out for Older Guys,* the author points out that a lot of older guys go after much younger girls because they think that it will be easier to manipulate and influence them. Do you

think that this is true? Do you think it is a good idea for younger girls to go out with much older guys? Why do you think that some guys go after underage girls instead of girls and women their own age? What are some of the problems that might come with dating a much older guy? What can girls your age do if an older guy does something that makes them uncomfortable or ties to get them to go out with them?

13.   In Power Move #33 *Know That Rainy Days Won't Last Forever*, the author points out that one of the best ways to turn a bad experience into a victory is to look at every challenge as an opportunity to learn and grow. What can we learn from a set back or challenge? Have you ever known anyone personally or on television who has come back stronger after a bad experience or mistake? What lessons can we take from the people that you have mentioned?

14.   Throughout *Cool, Confident and Strong*, Cassandra's underlying themes are: stand strong, follow your heart and be true to yourself. What can girls your age do to ensure that they stand strong during challenging times, pursue their dreams and stay true to themselves?

Tips for Starting Your Own Mother and Daughter Reading Group

- Check schools, libraries and community centers in your neighborhood to find out if a mother and daughter reading group exists.
- If none exists invite a group of friends who have daughters in the same age range and start your own group. If you have women who want to participate but do not have an adolescent daughter, ask them to bring a niece or consider mentoring an adolescent girl in need.
- Introduce mother-daughter teams, define group objectives, agree on group size, meeting locations, start and end times, how often the group will meet and what the host(s) responsibilities will be. You can have a different mother-daughter team host each meeting.
- Choose a group leader, someone who is committed to seeing the group succeed and who can keep the group moving forward as well as do the initial discussion group set-up.
- Allow daughters to choose half of the books, while mothers can choose the other half. Make sure that the books are age appropriate.
- Once titles are selected, have everyone purchase the book and read it by the next meeting date.

- Keep in mind that the book club is not school. It should not feel like it. It should be fun with the girls looking forward to coming to the meetings.
- Use a 10 to 15 minute fun icebreaker to begin each group meeting and a 10 minute closing activity to end each meeting.
- Distribute a members' list to everyone with names, addresses, telephone numbers and birthdays.

Suggestions for Your First Meeting

- As guests arrive, you and your daughter *(assuming the two of you are the first hosts)* should receive them with a warm welcome. You can have music playing in the background and maybe a photo album that they can look through while they are waiting for the other guests to arrive. Offer a beverage also while they wait.
- When all of your guests arrive, have them introduce themselves by telling the group their name, best movie they've seen this year, favorite group or artist and least favorite subject in school. You can also ask mother-daughter teams to bring a baby/much younger picture of themselves, put it on a poster board and have people take turns guessing who's who in each picture. Perhaps you can give a prize *(from the 99 cents store)* for the mother-daughter team that guesses the most correct responses.

- Begin the book discussion with each mother selecting a question from the *Cool, Confident and Strong* discussion guide or for other readings, make up your own questions and have the girls answer them in their own words.
- Serve snacks at the end. You can ask each mother-daughter team to whip up a snack or dish. Or you can allow the hosting mother-daughter team to prepare the snacks. Whatever works best for your group. And if there are leftovers, divide it among the group and let people take doggie bags.
- End with a 10 minute closing activity. You can have each daughter take turns selecting and leading the group in a closing activity. It should be light and fun like: create your own sundae party, a call and response song or poem, or the group can make something together. It's totally up to you. The goals are to bring mothers and daughters closer together through a hands-on activity and to allow group members to clear away any tension that might have arisen.
- Celebrate your accomplishments and schedule the next meeting.

Suggested Reading and Websites for Teen Girls

Books

❖ Am I The Last Virgin? by Tara Roberts

❖ Don't Give It Away by Iyanla Vanzant

❖ Girl Talk: All the Stuff Your Sister Never Told You by Carol Weston

❖ Got It Going On II: Power Tool for Girls by Janice Ferebe

❖ Ophellia Speaks: Adolescent Girls Write About Their Search for Self by Sara Shandler

❖ Taking Charge of My Mind and Body: A Girls Guide to Outsmarting Alcohol, Drugs, Smoking and Eating Problems by Gladys Folkers and Jeanne Engelmann

❖ Young, Gifted and Doing It: 52 Power Moves for Teens by Cassandra Mack. *(Available through mail order by photocopying the order form in the back of this book or you can purchase it on her website:* **www.empoweredliving.net**)

Websites

❖ *www.girlzone.com*
This website provides information and links about the latest fashions, travel, money management, trends and much more

❖ **www.girlsinc.org**
This is the official website of Girls Incorporated a national nonprofit organization that offers a multitude of programs for girls.

❖ **www.go-girl.com**
This website provides info about health and fitness, education, fashion and fun activities for girls

95

About the Author

Cassandra Mack, M.S.W. is a national workshop presenter and consultant who specializes in youth development, supervisory issues and the empowerment of girls and women. Her clients include: fortune 500 companies, schools, nonprofit organizations and churches.

Cassandra is the executive producer and host of, *The No More Drama Hour of Power,* a popular, call-in, internet, talk radio show of The New York Carib News.

Over the years, Cassandra has appeared on Good Day New York, Voices from the Village and What Woman Want. She has written articles for The Harlem Parent, Proud Poppa, The New York Beacon, and BELLE. She's been profiled in Black Enterprise and the Network Journal.

In addition to *Cool, Confident and Strong,* Cassandra has written a success guide for teens entitled, *Young, Gifted and Doing It.* She has also written two books for youth service professionals, *Smart Moves That Successful Youth Workers Make* and *Her Rite of Passage: How to Design and Deliver A Rites of Passage Program for African-American Girls and Young Women.*

Cassandra was born and raised in New York and has taken her powerful message of success and empowerment to youth and youth service professionals across the country. Cassandra received her Bachelor's degree in Speech from Brooklyn College and her Master's degree in Social Work from Hunter College.

For more information on Cassandra Mack's workshops and motivational programs or to listen to her weekly internet radio show go to: **www.strategiesforempoweredliving.com**

To book Cassandra to address your teens or staff, send an e-mail to our company at: **empoweredliving4u@yahoo.com**. Make sure to include the words *"Inquiring About Booking Cassandra,"* in the subject section of your email.

Other Books by Cassandra Mack

Cool, Confident and Strong: 52 Power Moves for Girls. ($12.95)
Give girls that tools they need to build healthy self-esteem and make smart dating and relationship choices.

Young, Gifted and Doing It: 52 Power Moves for Teens. ($14.95)
Give your teenagers the tools they need to succeed with this success guide for teens.

Smart Moves That Successful Youth Workers Make. ($24.95)
This book will show you how to become a highly effective youth worker. You'll learn: the seven functions of youth work and how to manage them, the eight most common mistakes that youth workers make and the eight smart moves of highly effective youth workers.

Her Rite of Passage: How to Design & Deliver A Rites of Passage Program for African-American Girls and Young Women. ($39.95)
This book will show you how to set up a rites of passage program from start to finish. It includes a 42-session workshop curriculum and step-by-step guidelines for planning and carrying out the initiation retreat and crossover ceremony.

978-0-595-47560-5
0-595-47560-4

Made in the USA
Lexington, KY
07 June 2016